When We All Wear a Mask

Reesa Shayne

Illustrated by Mehwish Aslam

Copyright © 2021 Reesa Shayne
All rights reserved

This book or any portion thereof may not be reproduced or used in any manner whatsoever without the express written permission of the author and publisher of the book except for brief use of quotations in a book review.

Written by Reesa Shayne
Illustrated by Mehwish Aslam

ISBN: 978-1-7366465-1-9

This book is dedicated to all first responders, medical professionals, healthcare workers, and their families.

THANK YOU for all that you do.

When I wear a mask,
I protect everyone I see.
And they protect me too.

My mom wears a mask.
My dad wears a mask.
My sister and brother do too.

It is different for sure, than playing was before. But it is something that we all should do.

If you wear a mask,
you help everyone you see
avoid getting icky and sick.

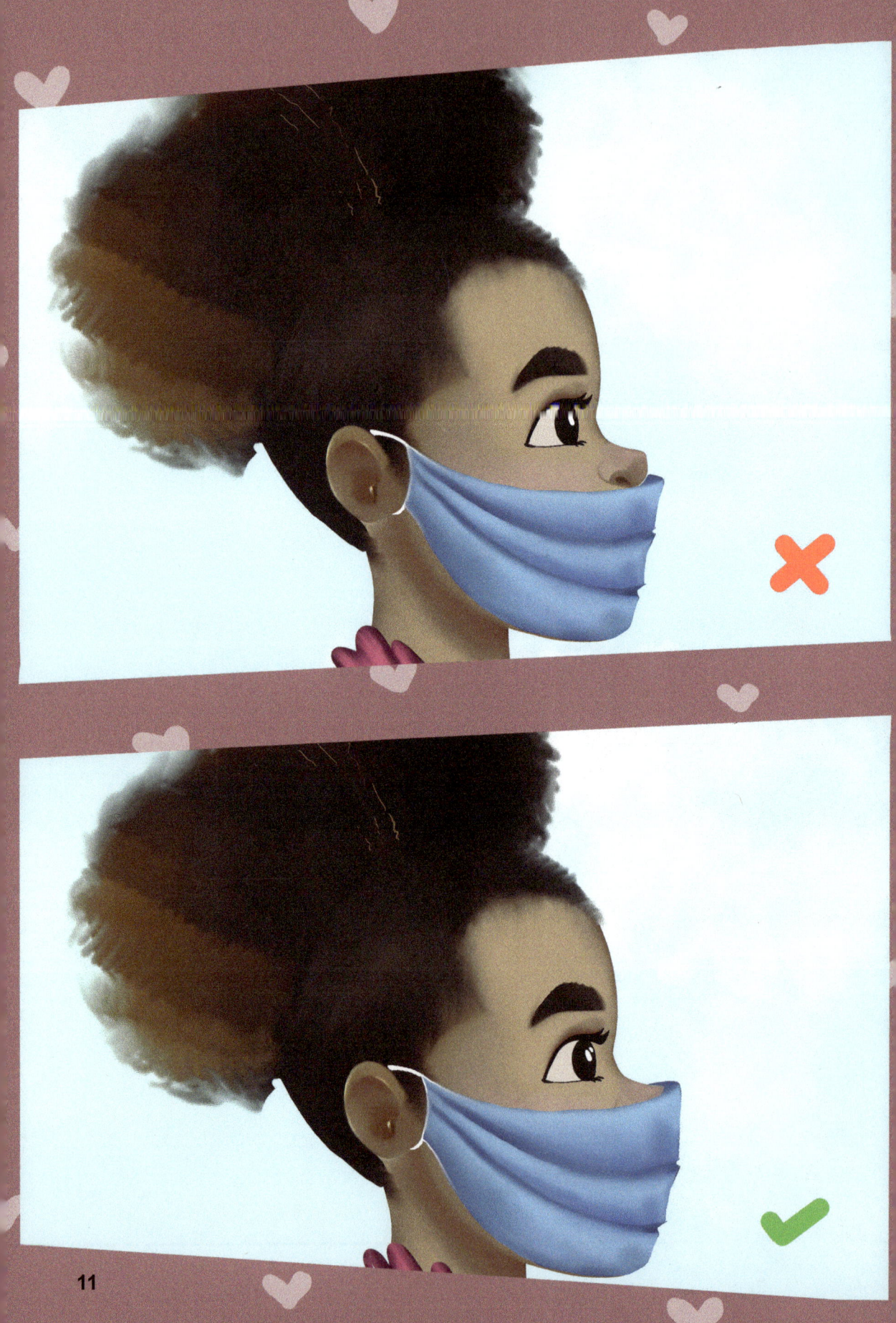

And make sure it covers your nose and your mouth. That is the most important trick!

When you are out,
and plan to see other friends,
always take your mask along
with you.

It is a small thing,
to remember to bring.
So important for me
and for you.

Thank you for wearing a mask.
Thank you for being a friend.
When we all wear a mask,
together, we win.

About the Author

Reesa Shayne is an African-American author dedicated to writing uplifting stories and diverse children's books. Her first children's book, **Polly Pear** published in 2018, is available as an e-book on all digital platforms along with companion activity books, **Color With Polly Pear** and **Write With Polly Pear**-a handwriting workbook.

After writing **When We All Wear A Mask**, Reesa immediately began working on her next children's book, which will be coming soon. You can learn even more about this author at ReesaShayneBooks.com and by following her on Instagram @ReesaShayneBooks and on Facebook at Facebook.com/ReesaShayne.

Thank You!

Thank you for purchasing this book!

Here are some of the ways to connect and follow me:

Website: www.reesashaynebooks.com

Twitter: @reesashayne

Facebook: @ReesaShayne

Instagram: @ReesaShayneBooks

Join my mailing list:
reesashaynebooks.com/subscribe

More Books by Reesa Shayne

Enjoyed this book? Check out these additional books from Reesa Shayne

Polly Pear

Description: Polly Pear is new in town, and nervous about making new friends. This heartwarming book encourages children to overcome their fears and be brave despite any nervous feelings they may have. Polly Pear is the first children's book from author Reesa Shayne, who will be bringing many more adventures and touching lessons to readers of all ages.

Color With Polly Pear

Description: If you absolutely loved the bright colors and images in the original Polly Pear story, then you will enjoy this coloring book! Get the best of both worlds in this coloring book for young readers to use their imagination and personality to color 26 fun pages while reading the sweet story of Polly Pear.

Write With Polly Pear – A Handwriting Workbook

Write with Polly Pear is a handwriting practice activity book for young readers. Based on the original Polly Pear story, this handwriting practice workbook gives young writers the opportunity to practice their handwriting skills with a positive, endearing story on being brave in new situations.

CPSIA information can be obtained
at www.ICGtesting.com
Printed in the USA
LVHW070850180321
681564LV00030B/1281